Cool Savory Muffins

Fun & Easy Baking Recipes for Kids!

Alex Kuskowski

Checkerboard
Library

An Imprint of Abdo Publishing
www.abdopublishing.com

visit us at www.abdopublishing.com

Published by Abdo Publishing, a division of ABDO,
PO Box 398166, Minneapolis, Minnesota 55439. Copyright © 2015
by Abdo Consulting Group, Inc. International copyrights reserved
in all countries. No part of this book may be reproduced in any
form without written permission from the publisher. Checkerboard
Library™ is a trademark and logo of Abdo Publishing.

Printed in the United States of America, North Mankato, Minnesota
062014
092014

THIS BOOK CONTAINS
RECYCLED MATERIALS

Editor: Karen Latchana Kenney
Content Developer: Nancy Tuminelly
Cover and Interior Design and Production:
Colleen Dolphin, Mighty Media, Inc.
Food Production: Frankie Tuminelly
Photo Credits: Colleen Dolphin, Shutterstock

The following manufacturers/names appearing in this
book are trademarks: Contadina®, Gold Medal®, Kemps®, Lunds &
Byerly's®, Old London®, Oscar Mayer®, PAM®, Quaker®, Roundy's®

Library of Congress Cataloging-in-Publication Data
Kuskowski, Alex, author.
   Cool savory muffins: fun & easy baking recipes for kids! /
Alex Kuskowski.
     pages cm. -- (Cool cupcakes & muffins)
   Audience: 8-12.
   Includes index.
   ISBN 978-1-62403-303-2
   1. Muffins--Juvenile literature. I. Title.
   TX770.M83K872 2015
   641.8'157--dc23
                    2013043082

To Adult Helpers

Assist a budding chef by
helping your child learn to cook.
Children develop new skills, gain
confidence, and make delicious
food when they cook. Some recipes
may be more difficult than others.
Offer help and guidance to your
child when needed. Encourage
creativity with recipes. Creative
cooking encourages children to
think like real chefs.

Before getting started, have ground
rules for using the kitchen, cooking
tools, and ingredients. There
should always be adult supervision
when a sharp tool, oven, or stove is
used. Be aware of the key symbols
described on page 9. They alert
you when certain things should be
monitored.

Put on your apron. Taste their
creations. Cheer on your new chef!

Contents

For the **Love** of Muffins!   4

The Basics   6

Cool Cooking Terms   8

Symbols   9

Kitchen Supplies   10

Ingredients   12

Super Savory Herb Pops   14

Mac & Cheesy Bites   16

Cheesy Pizza Puff Pieces   18

Surprising Corn Dog Bites   20

Hearty Eggs 'n' Bacon Brunch   22

Fluffy Potato Bake Bites   24

Chicken Pot Pie Surprise   26

Corn Bread Broccoli Muffins   28

Conclusion   30

Web Sites   30

Glossary   31

Index   32

For the Love of Muffins!

Muffins are for more than just breakfast! **Savory** muffins are muffins you can eat for dinner, lunch, or snacks. Muffins can also be tasty **versions** of your favorite meals.

The savory muffins in this book are quick to make. They are easy to eat too. Muffins are the perfect grab-and-go snacks! Try each of the recipes in this book. Or get creative and make up your own!

This book has everything you need to get started. It's filled with fun recipes. Follow each recipe's easy steps to create tasty treats. Get inspired to create muffins that taste and look great!

The Basics

Ask Permission

Before you cook, ask **permission** to use the kitchen, cooking tools, and ingredients. If you'd like to do something yourself, say so! Just remember to be safe. If you would like help, ask for it! Always ask when you are using a stove or oven.

Be Prepared

→ Be organized. Knowing where everything is makes cooking safer and more fun!

→ Read the directions all the way through before starting the recipe. Remember to follow the directions in order.

→ The most important ingredient is preparation! Make sure you have everything you'll need.

Be Neat and Clean

→ Start with clean hands, clean tools, and a clean work surface.

→ Tie back long hair to keep it out of the food.

→ Wear comfortable clothing and roll up your sleeves.

→ Put on an apron if you have one. It'll keep your clothes clean.

Measuring

Many ingredients are measured by the cup, tablespoon, or teaspoon. Measuring tools may come in many sizes, but the amount they measure should be printed or **etched** on the sides of the tools. When measuring 1 cup, use the measuring cup marked 1 cup and fill it to the top.

Some ingredients are measured by weight in ounces or pounds. The weight is printed on the package label.

Be Smart, Be Safe

→ Never cook if you are home alone.

→ Always have an adult nearby for hot jobs, such as ones that use the oven or the stove.

→ Have an adult around when using a sharp tool, such as a knife or a **grater**. Always be careful when using these tools!

→ Remember to turn pot handles toward the back of the stove. That way you avoid accidentally knocking the pots over.

No Germs Allowed!

Raw eggs and raw meat have bacteria in them. These bacteria are killed when the food is cooked. But bacteria can survive on things the food touched and that can make you sick! After you handle raw eggs or meat, wash your hands, tools, and work surfaces with soap and water. Keep everything clean!

Cool Cooking Terms

Here are some basic cooking terms and actions that go with them. Whenever you need a reminder, just turn back to these pages.

Wash

Always wash fruits and vegetables well. Rinse them under cold water. Pat them dry with a **towel**. Then they won't slip when you cut them.

Chop

Chop means to cut into small pieces.

Grate

Grate means to shred something into small pieces using a **grater**.

Slice

Slice means to cut food into pieces of the same thickness.

Symbols

Hot!

This recipe requires the use of a stove or oven. You will need adult **supervision** and assistance.

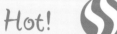

Sharp!

This recipe includes the use of a sharp **utensil** such as a knife or **grater**. Ask an adult to help out.

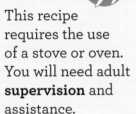

Kitchen Supplies

paper liners

small microwave-safe bowl

measuring cups

mini muffin tin

mixing bowls

measuring spoons

saucepan

cutting board

muffin tin

scoop

grater

plastic lollipop sticks

paper towels

mixing spoon

baking sheet

aluminum foil

colander

peeler

whisk

11

Ingredients

Here are some of the ingredients you will need:

cornmeal

all-purpose flour

bread crumbs

macaroni pasta

eggs

Yukon potatoes

whole milk

biscuit dough

pepperoni

pizza sauce

non-stick
cooking spray

bacon strips

hot dogs

green onions

buttermilk

vegetable
oil

cheddar
cheese

mozzarella
cheese

Parmesan
cheese

honey

Super Savory Herb Pops

MAKES 24 SERVINGS

Ingredients

non-stick cooking spray
1 cup all-purpose flour
½ tablespoon baking powder
½ teaspoon baking soda
¼ teaspoon salt
1 teaspoon dried oregano
1 teaspoon dried thyme

1 teaspoon dried basil
1 egg
½ cup buttermilk
1 tablespoon vegetable oil
1 teaspoon sugar
¼ cup grated cheddar cheese

Tools

mini muffin tin
measuring cups & spoons
grater
mixing bowls

mixing spoon
medium bowl
scoop

1   **Preheat** the oven to 400 degrees. Grease the muffin tin with non-stick cooking spray.

2   Put the flour, baking powder, baking soda, salt, oregano, thyme, and basil in a large mixing bowl. Stir.

3   Put the egg, buttermilk, oil, sugar, and cheese in a medium bowl. Stir.

4   Add the egg mixture to the flour mixture. Stir.

5   Fill the muffin cups two-thirds full of batter. Bake 15 minutes or until golden brown. Let the muffins cool.

Mac & Cheesy Bites

MAKES 12 SERVINGS

Ingredients

non-stick cooking spray
¾ cup bread crumbs
2 teaspoons olive oil
2 cups macaroni pasta
2 tablespoons unsalted butter

2 eggs
1 cup whole milk
½ cup grated Parmesan cheese
1 cup grated mozzarella cheese
1½ cups grated cheddar cheese

Tools

muffin tin
mixing bowls
measuring cups & spoons
mixing spoon

grater
saucepan
strainer

1   **Preheat** the oven to 350 degrees. Grease the muffin tin with non-stick cooking spray.

2   Put the bread crumbs and oil in a small mixing bowl. Stir.

3   Fill a saucepan with water. Bring it to a boil. Add the macaroni pasta. Cook 8 minutes. Drain the pasta.

4   Put the pasta in a medium bowl. Add the butter and eggs. Stir to coat the pasta. Add the milk, Parmesan cheese, mozzarella cheese, and 1 cup of cheddar cheese. Stir.

5   Fill the muffin cups with the pasta mixture. Sprinkle the remaining cheddar cheese and bread crumb mixture on top of the muffins. Bake 30 minutes or until light brown. Let the muffins cool.

Cheesy Pizza Puff Pieces

MAKES 24 SERVINGS

Ingredients

non-stick cooking spray
¾ cup all-purpose flour
¾ teaspoon baking powder
1 teaspoon dried oregano
½ teaspoon salt
¾ cup whole milk

1 egg
1 cup chopped pepperoni
1½ cups grated mozzarella
  cheese
½ cup pizza sauce

Tools

mini muffin tin
measuring cups & spoons
sharp knife
cutting board
grater

large mixing bowl
mixing spoon
whisk
small microwave-safe bowl

1   **Preheat** the oven to 375 degrees. Grease the muffin tin with non-stick cooking spray.

2   Put the flour, baking powder, oregano, and salt in a large mixing bowl. Stir.

3   Whisk in the milk and egg. Stir in the pepperoni and mozzarella. Let the batter sit 10 minutes.

4   Divide the batter evenly between the muffin cups. Bake 20 minutes.

5   Put the pizza sauce in a small bowl. Heat it in the microwave. Serve it with the Pizza Puff Pieces.

Surprising Corn Dog Bites

MAKES 12 SERVINGS

Ingredients

non-stick cooking spray
3 hot dogs
1¾ cups cornmeal
¾ cup all-purpose flour
1 tablespoon baking powder
1 teaspoon baking soda

½ teaspoon salt
¼ cup honey
½ cup buttermilk
2 eggs
¼ cup vegetable oil
ketchup

Tools

mini muffin tin
sharp knife
cutting board
mixing bowls

measuring cups & spoons
mixing spoon
plastic lollipop sticks

1   **Preheat** the oven to 425 degrees. Grease the muffin tin with non-stick cooking spray. Slice the hot dogs into ½-inch pieces.

2   Put the cornmeal, flour, baking powder, baking soda, and salt in a medium mixing bowl. Stir. Put the honey, buttermilk, eggs, and oil in a large bowl. Stir. Add the cornmeal mixture to the honey mixture. Stir.

3   Put 1 tablespoon of batter in each muffin cup. Place a hot dog piece in the center of each cup. Cover each hot dog piece with another tablespoon of batter.

4   Bake 14 minutes or until light brown. Let the muffins cool 5 minutes.

5   Push a lollipop stick into the top of each muffin. Serve with ketchup as a dipping sauce.

Hearty Eggs 'n' Bacon Brunch

MAKES 10 SERVINGS

Ingredients

non-stick cooking spray
4 bacon strips
1 10-oz. can biscuit dough
½ cup grated mozzarella cheese
3 eggs

2 tablespoons whole milk
½ teaspoon salt
½ teaspoon pepper
½ teaspoon oregano

Tools

baking sheet
aluminum foil
muffin tin
sharp knife

cutting board
medium mixing bowl
measuring cups & spoons
whisk

1   **Preheat** the oven to 400 degrees. Line the baking sheet with foil. Grease the muffin tin with non-stick cooking spray.

2   Lay the bacon strips flat on the baking sheet. Bake 15 minutes or until golden brown. Let the bacon cool. Chop the bacon into pieces.

3   Separate the biscuits. Push one into each muffin cup. Press the dough to the sides of the cups. Leave a small ridge around the edge of each cup. Divide the cheese evenly between muffin cups.

4   In a medium mixing bowl, whisk together the eggs, milk, salt, pepper, and oregano. Fill each muffin cup halfway with the egg mixture. Sprinkle the bacon on top of the muffins.

5   Bake 12 minutes or until light brown. Serve the muffins while they're still warm.

Fluffy Potato Bake Bites

Ingredients

3 Yukon potatoes
3 tablespoons unsalted butter
½ cup whole milk
4 tablespoons chopped
   green onions

½ cup grated Parmesan cheese
3 eggs
1 teaspoon salt
¼ teaspoon pepper

Tools

muffin tin
paper liners
peeler
sharp knife
cutting board

measuring cups & spoons
saucepan
strainer
large mixing bowl
fork

1   **Preheat** the oven to 400 degrees. Put paper liners in the muffin cups.

2   Peel and chop the potatoes. Fill a saucepan with water. Bring it to a boil. Add the potatoes. Cook 20 minutes. Drain the potatoes. Put them in a large mixing bowl.

3   Mash the potatoes with a fork until they are smooth.

4   Stir in the butter, milk, green onions, cheese, eggs, salt, and pepper.

5   Fill the muffin cups halfway with batter. Bake 20 minutes. Let the muffins cool.

Chicken
Pot Pie
Surprise

MAKES 10 SERVINGS

Ingredients

non-stick cooking spray
2 tablespoons vegetable oil
1 cup chopped chicken breast
1 10-oz. can biscuit dough
1 8-oz. can cream of chicken
    soup

⅔ cup grated cheddar cheese
1 cup frozen mixed vegetables
1 teaspoon onion powder
¼ teaspoon pepper

Tools

muffin tin
measuring cups & spoons
frying pan
sharp knife

cutting board
medium mixing bowl
mixing spoon
scoop

1   **Preheat** the oven to 400 degrees. Grease the muffin tin with non-stick cooking spray.

2   Put 1 tablespoon of oil in a frying pan. Heat it over medium-high heat. Add the chicken. Stir and cook 7 minutes. When the chicken is no longer pink, remove it from the heat. Let the chicken cool.

3   Separate the biscuits. Push one into each muffin cup. Press the dough to the sides of the cups. Leave a small ridge around the edge of each cup.

4   Put the chicken, soup, cheddar cheese, vegetables, onion powder, pepper, and remaining oil in a medium mixing bowl. Stir.

5   Divide the batter evenly between the muffin cups. Bake 12 minutes or until golden brown. Serve the muffins while they're still warm.

Corn Bread Broccoli Muffins

Ingredients

non-stick cooking spray
15 broccoli florets
1¾ cups cornmeal
¾ cup flour
4 teaspoons baking powder
¼ teaspoon baking soda

1 teaspoon salt
¼ cup sugar
1 teaspoon turmeric
2 cups buttermilk
2 eggs
¼ cup vegetable oil

Tools

two muffin tins
measuring cups & spoons
saucepan
strainer

paper towel
mixing bowls
mixing spoon

1 **Preheat** the oven to 400 degrees. Grease the muffin tins with non-stick cooking spray.

2 Fill a saucepan with water. Bring it to a boil. Add the broccoli. Cook 3 minutes. Drain the broccoli and let it cool. Pat the broccoli dry with a paper **towel**.

3 Put the cornmeal, flour, baking powder, baking soda, salt, sugar, and turmeric in a large mixing bowl. Stir.

4 Put the buttermilk, eggs, and oil in a small bowl. Stir. Add the buttermilk mixture to the cornmeal mixture. Stir.

5 Put 1 tablespoon of batter in each muffin cup. Place a broccoli floret in the center of each cup. Cover each broccoli floret with 2 tablespoons of batter.

6 Bake 15 to 18 minutes or until golden brown. Serve the muffins while they're still warm.

Conclusion

Savory muffins don't taste sweet. But they can be **delicious**. Making savory muffins doesn't have to be hard. It can be easy and fun!

This book has tons of fun recipes to get you started. There's more to discover too. Check your local library for more muffin cookbooks. Or use your imagination and whip up your very own creations!

Make muffins for any occasion. Your friends and family will love tasting your freshly baked recipes. Become a muffin tin chef today!

Web Sites

To learn more about cool cooking, visit ABDO online at www.abdopublishing.com. Web sites about cool cooking are featured on our Book Links page. These links are monitored and updated to provide the most current information available.

Glossary

delicious – very pleasing to taste or smell.

etch – to carve into something.

grater – a tool with rough-edged holes used to shred something into small pieces.

permission – when a person in charge says it's okay to do something.

preheat – to heat an oven to a certain temperature before putting in the food.

savory – having a strong, pleasing flavor that is not sweet.

supervision – the act of watching over or directing others.

towel – a cloth or paper used for cleaning or drying.

utensil – a tool used to prepare or eat food.

version – a different form or type from the original.

Index

A

adult helpers, guidelines
for, 2

B

bacon–biscuit muffins,
recipe for, 22–23

bacteria, in raw eggs and
meat, 7

C

cheese muffins, recipe for,
16–17

chicken muffins, recipe for,
26–27

cleanliness, guidelines for,
6, 7

cooking terms, 8

corn bread–broccoli muffins,
recipe for, 28–29

corn dog muffins, recipe for,
20–21

creativity, in cooking, 2, 4

H

herb muffins, recipe for,
14–15

I

ingredients
measuring of, 7
preparing of, 6
types of, 12–13

K

kitchen supplies, 10–11

kitchen use
permission for, 6
rules for, 2

M

measuring, tools for, 7

P

pizza muffins, recipe for,
18–19

potato muffins, recipe for,
24–25

preparation, for cooking, 6

R

recipes, reading and
following, 4, 6, 9

resources, about making
muffins, 30

S

safety, guidelines for, 2, 6, 7, 9

symbols, with recipes, 9

V

variety, in muffins, 4

W

Web sites, about cooking, 30